AMAZING SNAKES!

DEATH ADDERS

BY DAVY SWEAZEY

EPIC

BELLWETHER MEDIA • MINNEAPOLIS, MN

EPIC BOOKS are no ordinary books. They burst with intense action, high-speed heroics, and shadows of the unknown. Are you ready for an Epic adventure?

This edition first published in 2014 by Bellwether Media, Inc.

No part of this publication may be reproduced in whole or in part without written permission of the publisher. For information regarding permission, write to Bellwether Media, Inc., Attention: Permissions Department, 5357 Penn Avenue South, Minneapolis, MN 55419.

Library of Congress Cataloging-in-Publication Data

Sweazey, Davy, author.
  Death Adders / by Davy Sweazey.
    pages cm. – (Epic. Amazing Snakes!)
  Summary: "Engaging images accompany information about death adders. The combination of high-interest subject matter and light text is intended for students in grades 2 through 7"– Provided by publisher.
  Audience: 7-12.
  Includes bibliographical references and index.
  ISBN 978-1-62617-091-9 (hardcover : alk. paper)
  1. Acanthophis–Juvenile literature. 2. Snakes–Juvenile literature. I. Title.
  QL666.O64S94 2014
  597.96'4–dc23
                        2013035919

Printed in the United States of America, North Mankato, MN.

TABLE OF CONTENTS

WHAT ARE DEATH ADDERS?

Death adders are among the most venomous snakes in the world. They have thick bodies and wide heads. They grow up to 35 inches (90 centimeters) long.

4

What Did You Say?

Death adders may have first been called deaf adders. They cannot hear most sounds.

7

WHERE DEATH ADDERS LIVE

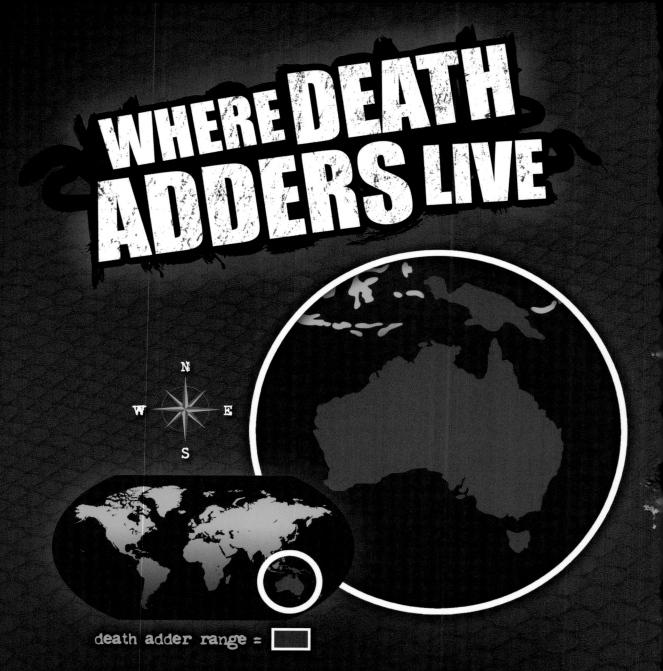

N
W   E
S

death adder range =

Death adders live in Australia and New Guinea. They often stay **coiled** on the ground. The snakes use **scutes** to slither.

7

Many death adders hide under fallen leaves in forests and grasslands. Others blend into sand in the desert. Their scales are brown, red, or gray to camouflage them.

AVOIDING PREDATORS

Death adders have few **predators**. Wild foxes, cats, and pigs are animals that do hunt them.

LURING PREY

Death adders **ambush** their **prey**. They attack birds, lizards, and **rodents**.

Food Poisoning

Sometimes an adder attracts dangerous prey. A death adder that eats a poisonous cane toad will die.

Death Adder Prey

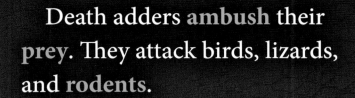

13

Sneak Attack

Death adders strike faster than any other venomous snake in Australia.

Death adders wiggle their tails to **lure** hungry animals. They wait for prey to get close. Then they **strike**!

The bite of a death adder is deadly for prey. Special teeth called **fangs** deliver **venom** into the animal. The venom makes the prey unable to move. It dies soon after.

Death adders stretch their **flexible** jaws. Then their whole meal slides into their belly!

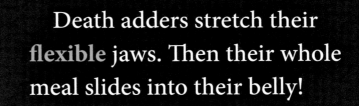

Wait and See
Death adders often wait for many days before an animal is within striking distance.

SPECIES PROFILE

SCIENTIFIC NAME:	*ACANTHOPHIS*
COMMON NAMES:	COMMON DEATH ADDER, NORTHERN DEATH ADDER, DESERT DEATH ADDER, PILBARA DEATH ADDER, ROUGH-SCALED DEATH ADDER
AVERAGE SIZE:	18-35 INCHES (45-90 CENTIMETERS)
HABITATS:	FORESTS, GRASSLANDS, COASTAL AREAS, DESERTS
COUNTRIES:	AUSTRALIA, INDONESIA, PAPUA NEW GUINEA
VENOMOUS:	YES
HUNTING METHOD:	AMBUSH, VENOMOUS BITE
COMMON PREY:	FROGS, LIZARDS, BIRDS, RODENTS

GLOSSARY

ambush—to attack by surprise

camouflage—to hide an animal by helping it blend in with the surroundings

coiled—looped around

fangs—sharp, hollow teeth; venom flows through fangs and into a bite.

flexible—able to stretch

lure—to attract

predators—animals that hunt other animals for food

prey—animals that are hunted by other animals for food

rodents—small animals that usually gnaw on their food

scales—small plates of skin that cover and protect a snake's body

scutes—large, rough scales on the stomach of a snake

strike—to bite quickly and with force

venom—a poison created by a snake; snakes use venom to hurt or kill other animals.

venomous—able to create venom in their bodies; death adders release venom through their fangs.

TO LEARN MORE

At the Library

Frazel, Ellen. *Adders*. Minneapolis, Minn.: Bellwether Media, 2012.

McCarthy, Colin. *Reptile*. New York, N.Y.: DK Pub., 2012.

White, Nancy. *Death Adders: Super Deadly!* New York, N.Y.: Bearport Pub., 2009.

On the Web

Learning more about death adders is as easy as 1, 2, 3.

1. Go to www.factsurfer.com.

2. Enter "death adders" into the search box.

3. Click the "Surf" button and you will see a list of related Web sites.

With factsurfer.com, finding more information is just a click away.

INDEX

The images in this book are reproduced through the courtesy of: fivespots, front cover, pp. 20-21; Robert Valentic/ Nature Picture Library, pp. 4-5, 7; Martin Willis/ Minden Pictures, pp. 8-9; Animals Animals/ SuperStock, p. 10; Eric Isselee, p. 11; NHPA/ SuperStock, pp. 12-13, 17, 18-19; Johan Larson, p. 13 (top); Sherjaca, p. 13 (middle); CreativeNature, p. 13 (bottom); Brooke Whatnall, pp. 14-15; Ian Waldie/ Getty Images, p. 16.